A Numerology Series

by

Lloyd Leon

NINE

Life Path Nine

Contents

Chapter 1

Understanding Life Path 9

The Numerology of Life Path 9

The Numerology of Life Path 9 reveals a profound tapestry of characteristics and potential that defines those who resonate with this life path. Individuals on this journey are often seen as compassionate, altruistic, and deeply empathetic. They possess an innate desire to serve humanity and make the world a better place, reflecting the essence of universal love and understanding. This life path is characterized by a strong sense of responsibility towards others, often leading individuals to engage in humanitarian efforts and social causes. Understanding these traits can help Life Path 9 individuals unlock their potential and embrace their true calling.

Emotional healing is a crucial theme for those on Life Path 9. They experience the world with heightened sensitivity, which can lead to deep emotional experiences and challenges. However, this sensitivity also provides a powerful avenue for healing, both for themselves and others. By engaging in practices such as meditation, journaling, or therapy, individuals can explore their emotional depths, ultimately leading to personal growth and self-discovery. This journey of healing is not only beneficial for Life Path 9 individuals but also allows them to extend their healing energy to those around them, reinforcing their role as emotional nurturers.

Life Path 9 individuals are often drawn to creative expression as a means of communicating their unique perspectives and feelings. This creative outlet can take many forms, such as art, music, writing, or activism. Engaging in creative endeavors allows them to channel their emotions productively, helping to alleviate the weight of their sensitivities. Furthermore, their artistic expressions often resonate with others, fostering a sense of connection and community. By tapping into their creativity, Life Path 9 individuals can find fulfillment and purpose, while also inspiring those around them to embrace their own journeys.

In the context of career and work environments, Life Path 9 individuals thrive in roles that allow them to contribute to the greater good. They are naturally inclined towards professions in social work, counseling, teaching, or any field that promotes humanitarian efforts. However, they may encounter challenges in traditional corporate settings where their idealism conflicts with profit-driven motives. Embracing their unique attributes can lead to fulfilling career paths that align with their values and allow them to make a meaningful impact in the world.

Spiritual growth and development are integral to the Life Path 9 experience. This journey often involves seeking deeper understanding and connection with the universe. By exploring various spiritual practices, such as mindfulness, yoga, or energy healing, individuals can cultivate a sense of inner peace and align with their higher purpose. Additionally, relationships and compatibility play a significant role in their spiritual journey. Life Path 9 individuals benefit from surrounding themselves with supportive, like-minded individuals who encourage their growth and understanding. In this way, they can navigate challenges, embrace forgiveness, and ultimately find deeper meaning and purpose in their lives.

Characteristics of Life Path 9 Individuals

Life Path 9 individuals are often characterized by their deep empathy and compassion for others. This innate ability to feel and understand the emotions of those around them makes them natural healers and caregivers. They are drawn to humanitarian efforts, seeking to alleviate suffering and promote social justice. This drive often leads them to engage in various charitable activities, where their desire to make a positive impact in the world can be fully realized. Their strong sense of idealism fuels their passion for advocating for causes that resonate with their values, making them prominent figures in movements focused on human rights, environmental sustainability, and community development.

Another defining characteristic of Life Path 9 individuals is their creative expression. Often gifted in the arts, they possess a unique ability to channel their feelings into various forms of creativity, whether it be writing, painting, or performing. This creative outlet not only serves as a means of self-expression but also acts as a therapeutic tool, enabling them to navigate their emotional landscapes. Their artistic endeavors often reflect their desire to inspire and provoke thought, allowing them to connect with others on a deeper level. Through their creativity, they can convey messages of hope and healing, resonating with those who share their vision of a better world.

Life Path 9 individuals are also known for their strong sense of purpose and the quest for spiritual growth. Many feel a calling to explore their spirituality, often engaging in practices that foster emotional healing and self-discovery. This journey often leads them to seek out teachings and philosophies that align with their innate desire for deeper understanding. They may gravitate towards meditation, yoga, or other spiritual practices that promote inner peace and clarity. This exploration not only enhances their self-awareness but also equips them with the tools necessary to guide others on their own paths to healing and enlightenment.

In relationships, Life Path 9 individuals are typically nurturing and supportive partners. Their ability to empathize allows them to form deep connections and foster a sense of belonging. However, they may face challenges in setting boundaries, often prioritizing the needs of others over their own. This tendency can lead to emotional burnout if not managed properly. Recognizing the importance of self-care is crucial for Life Path 9 individuals to maintain healthy relationships. By learning to balance their compassionate nature with their own needs, they can create fulfilling partnerships that honor both their aspirations and their commitments to others.

Finally, Life Path 9 individuals often encounter obstacles that challenge their ideals and sense of purpose. These challenges can manifest as feelings of frustration or disillusionment when the world does not align with their vision of what should be. Overcoming these hurdles requires resilience and a commitment to personal development. Engaging in practices that foster forgiveness, both towards themselves and others, can be transformative. By letting go of past grievances and focusing on their higher purpose, Life Path 9 individuals can find renewed strength and clarity, empowering them to continue their journey of making a meaningful impact on the world.

The Global Perspective of Life Path 9

Life Path 9 individuals are known for their deep humanitarian instincts, making their global perspective particularly unique and significant. This life path resonates with the ideals of universal love, compassion, and selflessness. As people who often feel a sense of responsibility towards the world, Life Path 9s tend to engage deeply with social causes, advocating for justice and equality. Their ability to see the interconnectedness of all beings fosters a profound understanding that personal growth is tied to the welfare of others. This perspective encourages them to contribute to global movements that aim for systemic change, whether through volunteering, activism, or supporting various humanitarian efforts.

Emotional healing is another crucial aspect of the Life Path 9 experience. This journey often invites individuals to confront their own emotional wounds to better serve others.

Through the lens of a global perspective, Life Path 9s understand that collective healing is essential for societal progress. Their empathic nature allows them to resonate with the suffering of others, which can be both a blessing and a challenge. By embracing their own healing processes, Life Path 9s can transform pain into purpose, using their experiences to inspire and uplift those around them. This journey not only aids in their personal development but also positions them as beacons of hope and healing in a world that often feels fractured.

In the realm of creative expression, Life Path 9s possess a unique ability to channel their insights into art, writing, and other creative outlets. This expression often serves as a medium for addressing global issues, allowing them to communicate complex feelings and thoughts in ways that resonate with a diverse audience. The global perspective enhances their creativity, enabling them to draw inspiration from various cultures and experiences. As they explore their artistic talents, they also tap into a deeper understanding of humanity, creating works that not only reflect personal truths but also highlight shared struggles and aspirations. This creative engagement can be a powerful tool for social change, as it encourages dialogue and fosters community.

Career paths for Life Path 9 individuals often align with their altruistic values. Many find fulfillment in professions that prioritize service over profit, such as social work, education, or non-profit leadership. Their global perspective drives them to seek careers that allow for significant contributions to society. In the workplace, they are often seen as natural leaders and mediators, skilled at bringing people together for a common cause. However, they may also face challenges in balancing their own needs with their desire to help others. Recognizing the importance of self-care and setting boundaries is essential for Life Path 9s to sustain their energies while pursuing their vocational callings.

Spiritual growth and development are integral to the Life Path 9 journey, often manifesting in a quest for deeper meaning and purpose. This exploration frequently leads them to study various spiritual traditions and philosophies, fostering a rich understanding of global spirituality. Life Path 9s are naturally inclined to ponder existential questions, seeking answers that transcend cultural boundaries. By embracing diverse spiritual practices, they can cultivate a holistic approach to their personal development. The lessons learned along this path empower them to forgive not only others but also themselves, ultimately leading to a sense of liberation and fulfillment. Through this journey, Life Path 9s find their place in the world, not just as individuals, but as vital contributors to the collective human experience.

Chapter 2

Unlocking the Potential of Life Path 9

Embracing Unique Traits

Embracing unique traits is essential for individuals on Life Path 9, as it allows them to tap into their inherent gifts and contribute meaningfully to the world. Those on this path often possess a deep sense of compassion, creativity, and a desire to serve humanity. Recognizing and honoring these traits enables Life Path 9 individuals to align with their true selves, fostering a sense of fulfillment and purpose. By understanding the unique qualities that define them, they can transform challenges into opportunities for growth and self-discovery.

One of the most significant aspects of Life Path 9 is the ability to empathize with others. This emotional intelligence is a powerful tool that can lead to profound connections and healing in relationships. By embracing their empathetic nature, Life Path 9 individuals can become effective communicators and healers, supporting those around them in their journeys. This deep connection not only enhances personal relationships but also fuels their humanitarian efforts, allowing them to advocate for social justice and contribute to causes that resonate with their values.

Creativity is another hallmark trait of Life Path 9 individuals. Whether through art, writing, music, or other forms of expression, they have an innate ability to channel their emotions into creative outlets. Embracing this creative aspect is crucial for personal growth and emotional healing. It allows them to process their experiences and share their unique perspectives with the world. Engaging in creative expression not only nurtures their soul but also inspires others, fostering a sense of community and collaboration among like-minded individuals.

In the realm of career and work environments, Life Path 9 individuals often thrive in roles that allow them to make a difference. Embracing their unique traits can lead to fulfilling careers in fields such as social work, counseling, art therapy, or non-profit organizations. Their natural inclination towards service and leadership can guide them to positions where they can inspire and uplift others. By seeking out environments that resonate with their values, they can harness their gifts to create meaningful change in their workplaces and beyond.

Lastly, embracing unique traits paves the way for spiritual growth and personal development. Life Path 9 individuals are often on a quest for deeper understanding and purpose. By acknowledging their gifts and working through their challenges, they can cultivate a strong sense of self-awareness. This journey often involves recognizing the power of forgiveness, both for themselves and others, enabling them to release past burdens and embrace a more authentic existence. By fully embracing their unique traits, Life Path 9 individuals can unlock their potential and embark on a transformative journey towards self-discovery and fulfillment.

Developing Emotional Intelligence

Developing emotional intelligence is a vital aspect of the journey for those on Life Path 9, as it aligns closely with their innate desire to serve humanity and connect deeply with others. Emotional intelligence encompasses the ability to recognize, understand, and manage one's own emotions while also empathizing with the emotions of others. For Life Path 9 individuals, who often prioritize the well-being of others, cultivating this skill can be transformative. By enhancing their emotional intelligence, they can navigate their personal relationships and humanitarian efforts more effectively, fostering deeper connections and promoting healing.

The journey of developing emotional intelligence begins with self-awareness. Life Path 9 individuals are often introspective, which can be a double-edged sword. While this introspection aids in understanding their own feelings, it can also lead to emotional overwhelm. By practicing mindfulness and engaging in reflective activities such as journaling or meditation, Life Path 9 individuals can gain clarity about their emotions. This self-awareness allows them to identify emotional triggers and patterns, creating a foundation for healthier responses in various situations, whether in personal relationships or professional environments.

Another critical component of emotional intelligence is self-regulation. Life Path 9 individuals may encounter challenges that evoke strong emotional responses, especially when faced with injustices or suffering in the world. Learning to manage these emotions constructively is essential. Techniques such as deep breathing, grounding exercises, and positive visualization can help them maintain composure during stressful times. By mastering self-regulation, they not only enhance their emotional well-being but also become role models for others, demonstrating how to respond to adversity with grace and resilience.

Empathy is a hallmark of emotional intelligence, and for Life Path 9 individuals, it is particularly significant. Their deep sensitivity often enables them to feel the pain and joy of others, making them natural healers and advocates. Strengthening this empathy involves actively listening to others without judgment and seeking to understand their perspectives. Engaging in volunteer work or humanitarian efforts can further enhance this skill, as it provides opportunities to connect with diverse communities. As they cultivate empathy, Life Path 9 individuals can create meaningful relationships that enrich their lives and those around them.

Finally, developing emotional intelligence culminates in improved interpersonal skills and social awareness. Life Path 9 individuals can harness their emotional insights to foster collaboration and harmony in their interactions. By practicing open communication and conflict resolution techniques, they can navigate their relationships more effectively, whether in personal or professional settings. This growth not only aids their personal development but also amplifies their ability to contribute positively to society. Ultimately, by cultivating emotional intelligence, those on Life Path 9 can unlock their full potential, enhancing their journey of self-discovery and their impact on the world.

Cultivating Resilience

Cultivating resilience is a vital aspect of the journey for individuals on Life Path 9, who often face unique challenges due to their deep emotional sensitivity and humanitarian instincts. Resilience, defined as the ability to bounce back from adversity, is particularly crucial for Life Path 9 individuals, who may encounter emotional turmoil as they navigate their roles as healers and caregivers. By developing resilience, they can transform challenges into opportunities for growth, ultimately enhancing their capacity to serve others and contribute to the greater good.

One key strategy for cultivating resilience is embracing emotional healing. Life Path 9 individuals often carry the weight of collective suffering, which can lead to feelings of overwhelm and despair. Engaging in practices such as mindfulness, therapy, and creative expression allows them to process their emotions constructively. Journaling, art, and music can serve as powerful outlets for emotional release, enabling Life Path 9 individuals to channel their feelings into something meaningful. This transformative process not only alleviates emotional burdens but also strengthens their ability to cope with future adversities.

Furthermore, building a supportive community plays a significant role in fostering resilience. Life Path 9 individuals thrive in environments where they can connect with like-minded peers who share their vision for humanitarian efforts. By participating in group activities, volunteering, or joining support networks, they can cultivate a sense of belonging that reinforces their commitment to their mission. These connections provide encouragement during challenging times, reminding them that they are not alone and that their efforts are valued and impactful.

Another important aspect of resilience is the practice of forgiveness. Life Path 9 individuals often grapple with feelings of resentment or hurt from past experiences, which can impede their emotional growth. Learning to forgive, both themselves and others, is essential for breaking free from the chains of negativity that can hinder their progress. Forgiveness allows them to release emotional baggage and fosters a sense of peace that enhances their overall resilience. This practice not only aids in personal healing but also empowers them to approach their humanitarian goals with a renewed sense of purpose.

Ultimately, cultivating resilience is a continuous journey that empowers Life Path 9 individuals to embrace their unique gifts while navigating the complexities of life. By focusing on emotional healing, fostering community connections, and practicing forgiveness, they can enhance their ability to overcome challenges and fully realize their potential.

Resilience not only enriches their personal development but also amplifies their contributions to the world, allowing them to fulfill their roles as compassionate leaders and agents of change.

Chapter 3

Emotional Healing and Life Path 9

Recognizing Emotional Wounds

Recognizing emotional wounds is a crucial step for individuals on Life Path 9, as it allows for profound personal growth and healing. Life Path 9 individuals are often idealistic, compassionate, and deeply connected to the collective human experience. However, this sensitivity can also leave them vulnerable to emotional wounds that may stem from past relationships, societal injustices, or personal failures. Understanding these wounds is essential not only for healing but also for unlocking the unique gifts and potentials inherent in this life path. By acknowledging and processing these emotional scars, individuals can transform their pain into a source of strength and creativity.

Emotional wounds can manifest in various ways, including feelings of inadequacy, resentment, or a pervasive sense of disconnection from others. Life Path 9 individuals may find themselves grappling with a heightened sense of responsibility for the world's suffering, which can lead to burnout or feelings of helplessness. Recognizing these patterns is the first step toward healing. Journaling, introspection, and open discussions with trusted friends or therapists can facilitate this recognition, enabling individuals to pinpoint the origins of their emotional pain and how it affects their interactions and contributions to the world.

Furthermore, acknowledging emotional wounds allows Life Path 9 individuals to explore the deeper meanings behind their experiences. Often, these challenges are not just personal struggles but reflections of broader societal issues that resonate with their humanitarian instincts. By reframing their wounds as opportunities for understanding and connection, individuals can cultivate a greater sense of empathy, both for themselves and for others. This process is not only vital for personal healing but also for fostering a more compassionate society, aligning perfectly with the humanitarian essence of Life Path 9.

Creative expression serves as a powerful tool for recognizing and processing emotional wounds. Life Path 9 individuals often possess strong artistic inclinations, whether through writing, visual arts, or music. Engaging in creative activities can provide an outlet for emotions that may be difficult to articulate verbally. By channeling their experiences into creative forms, individuals can gain insights into their emotional wounds, transforming pain into art that resonates with others. This artistic journey not only facilitates personal healing but also contributes to the collective healing of the community, as their work can inspire and uplift those who share similar struggles.

In embracing the journey of recognizing emotional wounds, Life Path 9 individuals embark on a path of profound transformation. This process not only brings clarity and healing to their own lives but also enhances their ability to serve others. By confronting their emotional challenges, they can develop resilience and wisdom that enrich their humanitarian efforts. Ultimately, recognizing and healing emotional wounds becomes a pivotal aspect of their journey, allowing them to unlock their fullest potential and contribute meaningfully to the world around them.

Healing Through Self-Awareness

Healing through self-awareness is a transformative journey that resonates profoundly with individuals on Life Path 9. This path is often characterized by a deep sense of compassion, a desire to serve humanity, and a profound understanding of the interconnectedness of all beings. For Life Path 9 individuals, self-awareness acts as a powerful tool that not only aids in personal healing but also enhances their ability to contribute positively to the world around them. By cultivating self-awareness, they can identify and address emotional wounds, fostering a profound sense of inner peace and resilience.

Self-awareness begins with introspection, an essential practice for Life Path 9 individuals who often feel the weight of the world on their shoulders. By taking the time to reflect on their thoughts, feelings, and actions, they can uncover the underlying motivations that drive them. This process allows them to recognize patterns that may have caused emotional pain or hindered their personal growth. Through journaling, meditation, or quiet contemplation, Life Path 9 individuals can create a safe space for self-exploration, enabling them to confront and heal past traumas that may be holding them back.

As Life Path 9 individuals embrace their emotional healing journey, they often discover that their unique gift lies in their ability to empathize with others. This heightened sense of awareness not only brings clarity to their own experiences but also enhances their understanding of the struggles faced by those around them. By acknowledging their own emotional wounds, they become more compassionate and forgiving, both to themselves and to others. This shift in perspective is crucial for fostering healthy relationships, as it allows Life Path 9 individuals to form deeper connections built on mutual understanding and shared experiences.

Furthermore, self-awareness empowers Life Path 9 individuals to harness their creativity as a means of healing. Many people on this path possess artistic inclinations that serve as an outlet for their emotions. By engaging in creative expression—whether through art, music, writing, or other forms—they can channel their feelings into something tangible and healing. This process not only provides a sense of relief but also helps them articulate their experiences in a way that can inspire and uplift others. As they share their creative works with the world, they contribute to a greater understanding of the human experience, reinforcing their role as healers and humanitarians.

Ultimately, healing through self-awareness is a continuous journey for those on Life Path 9. It invites them to confront the challenges and obstacles they face with courage and vulnerability. By embracing their unique gifts and understanding their purpose in the grand tapestry of life, they can cultivate a profound sense of fulfillment. This journey not only leads to personal healing but also empowers them to make meaningful contributions to the world, aligning their actions with their values and aspirations. Through self-awareness, Life Path 9 individuals unlock their potential, embracing their role as beacons of light and hope in a world that often seeks healing.

Techniques for Emotional Release

Techniques for emotional release are essential for individuals on Life Path 9 as they navigate their unique journey of self-discovery and humanitarian efforts. This life path often involves deep emotional experiences and a heightened sensitivity to the world around them. To unlock the potential inherent in Life Path 9, one must engage in practices that facilitate the release of pent-up emotions, fostering healing and growth. Techniques such as journaling, meditation, and expressive arts are particularly beneficial, allowing individuals to process their feelings and gain clarity about their experiences.

Journaling serves as a powerful tool for emotional release, enabling Life Path 9 individuals to articulate their thoughts and feelings in a safe space. By writing down their emotions, they can confront and understand what lies beneath the surface. This practice not only promotes self-awareness but also helps in identifying patterns and triggers that may influence their emotional state. Regular journaling encourages a reflective process, allowing Life Path 9 individuals to document their growth and transformation over time, which is crucial for their overall emotional healing.

Meditation and mindfulness practices can significantly enhance emotional release for those on Life Path 9. Engaging in regular meditation helps calm the mind and body, creating an environment conducive to emotional exploration. Techniques such as guided visualization or breathwork can be particularly effective, as they allow individuals to connect with their inner selves and release emotional tension. By cultivating a state of presence, Life Path 9 individuals can better navigate their emotions, fostering resilience and promoting spiritual growth as they learn to embrace the lessons inherent in their emotional experiences.

Expressive arts, including music, dance, and visual arts, provide another avenue for emotional release that resonates deeply with Life Path 9 individuals. These creative outlets allow for the expression of feelings that may be difficult to articulate with words. Engaging in artistic endeavors can serve as a therapeutic process, helping individuals channel their emotions into something beautiful and meaningful. This form of expression not only aids in personal development but can also inspire others, aligning with the humanitarian spirit that characterizes Life Path 9.

Finally, incorporating practices of forgiveness into emotional release techniques is vital for those on Life Path 9. The power of forgiveness can lead to profound emotional healing and release longstanding burdens. By letting go of past grievances, individuals can clear space for new opportunities and relationships. Forgiveness is not just a gift to others; it is a gift to oneself, allowing Life Path 9 individuals to move forward with purpose and meaning. Embracing these techniques fosters a deeper understanding of their emotional landscape, empowering them to live authentically and contribute positively to the world around them.

Chapter 4

Life Path 9 and Humanitarian Efforts

The Call to Service

The Call to Service is an intrinsic part of the Life Path 9 journey. Individuals with this life path are often drawn to humanitarian efforts, feeling a profound sense of responsibility to contribute positively to society. This calling is not merely a desire to help others; it stems from a deep-seated understanding of interconnectedness and the shared human experience. Life Path 9 individuals possess a unique ability to empathize with the struggles of others, which often drives them to engage in service-oriented activities. This commitment to serving humanity can manifest in various forms, from volunteering and activism to creative expressions that raise awareness about social issues.

Emotional healing is another critical aspect of the Call to Service for Life Path 9 individuals. Their journey often involves personal struggles that lead to a heightened sensitivity towards the emotional pain of others. This empathetic nature allows them to connect deeply with those in need, making them effective healers and support systems within their communities. By sharing their own experiences and insights, Life Path 9 individuals can inspire others to confront their emotional challenges, fostering a culture of healing and resilience. This process not only aids others but also promotes their own emotional growth and understanding of life's complexities.

In the realm of creative expression, the Call to Service takes on a distinctive form. Life Path 9 individuals are often gifted artists, writers, and performers who use their talents to convey messages of hope, unity, and social change. Their work can serve as a catalyst for awareness and action, encouraging others to recognize their own potential for making a difference. Through creativity, they can articulate the struggles of marginalized communities and advocate for justice, thereby intertwining their artistic endeavors with their humanitarian impulses. This interplay between creativity and service enriches their lives and the lives of those who resonate with their messages.

Career paths for Life Path 9 individuals frequently reflect their calling to service. Many find themselves drawn to professions in social work, counseling, education, or non-profit organizations, where they can directly impact the lives of others. Their strong moral compass and desire for fulfillment often lead them to seek roles that align with their values. However, the journey is not without challenges. They may encounter obstacles such as burnout or feelings of inadequacy when faced with the enormity of social issues. Recognizing these challenges as part of their growth can empower Life Path 9 individuals to develop personal strategies for balance and renewal.

Ultimately, the Call to Service is a vital aspect of the Life Path 9 experience that encourages spiritual growth and personal development. Through acts of service, individuals not only uplift others but also embark on a journey of self-discovery and purpose. This path invites them to explore their values, confront their limitations, and cultivate a deeper understanding of forgiveness and compassion. By embracing their calling, Life Path 9 individuals can unlock their potential, transforming challenges into opportunities for growth and fostering a profound sense of meaning in their lives.

Activism and Advocacy

Activism and advocacy play a crucial role in the journey of Life Path 9 individuals, who are often seen as the humanitarian figures within the numerological framework. Those on this path are imbued with a deep sense of compassion and a desire to effect positive change in the world. Their innate ability to empathize with the struggles of others often motivates them to engage in causes that advocate for social justice, environmental sustainability, and the well-being of marginalized communities. By channeling their energies into activism, Life Path 9 individuals not only fulfill their purpose but also contribute significantly to the collective healing of society.

The emotional healing aspect of Life Path 9 is closely intertwined with their activism. Engaging in advocacy work allows these individuals to transform their personal pain into a force for good. Many Life Path 9s have experienced profound emotional challenges, and through their efforts to uplift others, they uncover a pathway to their own healing. This reciprocal relationship between personal growth and social activism empowers them to navigate their emotional landscapes while simultaneously addressing the issues that resonate with their values. As they advocate for the rights of others, they also find solace in shared experiences and foster connections that promote their emotional well-being.

Creative expression is another vital component of activism for Life Path 9 individuals. Their unique artistic talents often serve as a medium to convey powerful messages about the injustices they seek to rectify. Whether through writing, art, music, or performance, Life Path 9s can articulate the struggles of humanity in ways that resonate deeply with others. This creative outlet not only enriches their own lives but also inspires others to engage in advocacy. By using their gifts to raise awareness and provoke thought, they tap into their core essence and invite others to join them on transformative journeys toward social change.

In the context of career and work environments, Life Path 9 individuals thrive in roles that align with their values of compassion and service. This can manifest in various professions such as social work, education, or non-profit organizations. Their ability to understand and connect with the emotional needs of others makes them effective advocates in the workplace. They naturally gravitate toward environments that allow them to champion causes and support initiatives that reflect their humanitarian ideals. By fostering a culture of empathy and collaboration, they not only elevate their own careers but also inspire colleagues to embrace a more socially responsible approach to their work.

Finally, the spiritual growth and development of Life Path 9 individuals are deeply enriched through activism. As they engage with diverse communities and confront complex social issues, they are presented with opportunities for profound personal reflection and spiritual exploration. They learn to navigate the challenges of advocacy with grace and resilience, which enhances their understanding of forgiveness, purpose, and meaning in life. By embracing their role as advocates, Life Path 9s not only contribute to the betterment of society but also embark on a journey of self-discovery that ultimately leads to a more fulfilling and purposeful existence.

Making a Global Impact

Life Path 9 individuals are often seen as the humanitarians of the numerological spectrum, driven by a deep-seated desire to make a positive difference in the world. This intrinsic motivation stems from their compassionate nature, which allows them to empathize with the struggles of others. It is essential for those on this path to recognize that their unique gifts can be harnessed to create meaningful change, not just on a personal level, but on a global scale. By embracing their role as global citizens, Life Path 9 individuals can transform their emotional healing journeys into powerful acts of service that uplift both themselves and the communities they engage with.

The journey towards making a global impact involves understanding the interconnectedness of humanity. Life Path 9 individuals possess an innate ability to see the bigger picture, often feeling a sense of responsibility towards the collective well-being of society. This perspective can fuel their passion for humanitarian efforts, prompting them to engage in activities that address social issues, environmental challenges, and global injustices. Through volunteering, advocacy, or even initiating grassroots movements, those on this path can utilize their creative expression as a means to rally others and inspire collective action. The ability to communicate their vision effectively can turn ideas into realities, making their contributions invaluable.

Emotional healing plays a significant role in how Life Path 9 individuals can influence the world around them. By working through their own challenges and traumas, they cultivate resilience and wisdom that can guide others facing similar struggles. In sharing their stories and insights, they not only heal themselves but also serve as beacons of hope for those in need. This transformative process can lead to the establishment of support networks, workshops, or community programs that focus on healing and empowerment. Such initiatives can break down barriers, foster understanding, and promote unity, ultimately contributing to a more compassionate society.

In the professional realm, Life Path 9 individuals often find themselves drawn to careers that align with their values of service and creativity. Whether in nonprofit organizations, education, or the arts, their work can reflect their desire to enact change. By pursuing careers that resonate with their humanitarian spirit, they can infuse their day-to-day activities with purpose, making their contributions impactful. Additionally, cultivating relationships with like-minded individuals in their fields can enhance their ability to collaborate on projects that have far-reaching implications. Working together amplifies their efforts, creating a ripple effect that can inspire others to join in the mission.

Finally, spiritual growth is integral to the journey of Life Path 9 individuals as they seek to make a global impact. This path encourages them to explore various philosophies and practices that deepen their understanding of themselves and the world. By nurturing their spiritual development, they can uncover their true purpose and refine their vision for a better world. Engaging in self-discovery and personal development strategies not only empowers them but also equips them with the tools needed to face challenges and obstacles along the way. The power of forgiveness, both for themselves and others, becomes a crucial element in this process, allowing them to release past burdens and focus on their mission to create a brighter future for all.

Chapter 5

Creative Expression for Life Path 9 Individuals

Exploring Artistic Outlets

Artistic outlets serve as profound avenues for self-expression and healing, particularly for individuals on Life Path 9. This life path is characterized by a deep sense of compassion and a desire to make a difference in the world. Engaging in creative activities such as painting, writing, music, or dance allows those on this journey to channel their emotions, confront their inner struggles, and ultimately transform pain into beauty. The act of creating can be therapeutic, providing a safe space to process complex feelings and experiences, which is especially vital for Life Path 9 individuals who often bear the emotional weight of the world.

Through artistic expression, Life Path 9 individuals can tap into their innate talents while simultaneously contributing to the greater good. Their creativity often reflects their humanitarian spirit, as they seek to inspire others and raise awareness of social issues through their art. Whether it's through visual art that highlights injustice, writing that tells stories of resilience, or music that evokes empathy, these creative endeavors can serve as powerful tools for advocacy and change. This connection between art and activism not only enhances personal fulfillment but also aligns with their life purpose of serving humanity.

Moreover, engaging in the arts fosters emotional healing, a crucial aspect of the Life Path 9 experience. Many individuals on this path encounter emotional challenges, including feelings of isolation and a sense of being misunderstood. Artistic pursuits can provide a means of release, allowing for vulnerability and authenticity. By expressing their innermost thoughts and feelings through art, they can confront past traumas and work towards forgiveness, both for themselves and others. This process of emotional catharsis is essential for their personal growth and spiritual development.

In the context of career and work environments, Life Path 9 individuals often thrive in creative fields. Their innovative ideas and empathetic approach make them valuable assets in professions that require a blend of creativity and compassion, such as social work, teaching, or the arts. By aligning their careers with their passions, they not only find greater satisfaction in their professional lives but also continue to fulfill their life's mission of serving and uplifting others. This synergy between creativity and vocation is vital for maintaining a sense of purpose and direction.

Finally, artistic outlets can enhance relationships and interpersonal connections for those on Life Path 9. Sharing creative experiences with others fosters deeper bonds and understanding, allowing for meaningful exchanges that transcend superficial interactions. Collaborative artistic projects or simply enjoying art together can strengthen relationships and promote a sense of community. For Life Path 9 individuals, who often feel a calling to unite and heal, these shared experiences can be transformative, reinforcing their commitment to nurturing connections and contributing positively to the world around them.

The Healing Power of Creativity

Creativity serves as a profound avenue for emotional healing, particularly for individuals on Life Path 9. This life path is often characterized by a deep sense of empathy, compassion, and a desire to make a positive impact on the world. However, the emotional weight that comes with these traits can lead to feelings of overwhelm or even despair. Engaging in creative activities allows Life Path 9 individuals to channel their emotions constructively, transforming pain into art, music, writing, or other forms of expression. This process not only fosters personal healing but also creates a bridge to connect with others who may share similar struggles.

The act of creating can be therapeutic, offering a sanctuary where Life Path 9 individuals can explore their innermost thoughts and feelings without judgment. Whether through painting, sculpting, or composing music, the creative process allows for a release of pent-up emotions, facilitating clarity and understanding. This self-exploration is essential for emotional healing, as it encourages individuals to

31

confront their past experiences and traumas, ultimately leading to acceptance and growth. Engaging in creativity helps Life Path 9 individuals articulate their feelings, making it easier to navigate their complex emotional landscape.

Moreover, creativity can serve as a powerful tool for humanitarian efforts, which resonate deeply with the values of Life Path 9. Many individuals on this path feel a strong calling to contribute to the greater good, and creative expression can amplify their message and impact. Projects that combine artistic endeavors with social causes not only enrich the lives of those involved but also foster a sense of community and shared purpose. By harnessing their creative gifts, Life Path 9 individuals can inspire others, raise awareness, and advocate for change, thus realizing their potential as catalysts for healing in the world.

In career and work environments, embracing creativity can lead to fulfilling and meaningful professional paths for Life Path 9 individuals. Many find themselves drawn to careers in the arts, education, or social services, where they can utilize their creativity to inspire and uplift others. By integrating creative thinking into their work, they can develop innovative solutions to challenges, cultivate collaborative atmospheres, and enhance overall job satisfaction. This not only benefits their personal development but also creates a positive ripple effect within their organizations and communities.

Ultimately, the healing power of creativity is intertwined with the spiritual growth and development of Life Path 9 individuals. As they engage with their creative side, they embark on a journey of self-discovery that deepens their understanding of themselves and their purpose in life. The process of creating encourages introspection and mindfulness, allowing individuals to connect with their inner selves and the universe around them. This connection is vital for fostering forgiveness, overcoming challenges, and finding meaning in life's experiences. By unlocking the gifts of creativity, Life Path 9 individuals can cultivate a fulfilling and enriched life, grounded in healing and purpose.

Channeling Emotions into Art

Channeling emotions into art can be a profound avenue for Life Path 9 individuals, who often grapple with deep feelings and a strong sense of empathy. As natural humanitarians, those on this path frequently encounter emotional experiences that can be both overwhelming and enlightening. Engaging in artistic expression allows them to transform raw emotions into tangible forms, whether through painting, writing, music, or other creative outlets. This process not only serves as a therapeutic release but also enables Life Path 9 individuals to connect with others, fostering a sense of community and shared understanding through their art.

Artistic expression can be particularly beneficial for emotional healing. Life Path 9 individuals may carry the weight of their experiences, often feeling the pain and joy of others as well. By channeling these emotions into their art, they can process their feelings in a constructive manner. This creative outlet becomes a safe space where they can explore their inner world, confront unresolved emotions, and ultimately find clarity and peace. The act of creating can help them navigate their emotional landscapes, transforming pain into beauty and fostering resilience in the face of life's challenges.

Furthermore, the humanitarian instincts of Life Path 9 individuals can be amplified through their artistic endeavors. By using their art to address social issues or to advocate for change, they can bring attention to causes close to their hearts. This can be a powerful form of activism, allowing them to use their gifts to uplift others and promote healing within communities. Their creativity becomes a vehicle for compassion, enabling them to express their values and inspire others to engage in humanitarian efforts. In this way, art serves not only as a personal outlet but also as a platform for collective change.

In the realm of career and work environments, channeling emotions into art can enhance professional fulfillment for Life Path 9 individuals. Many find themselves drawn to careers in creative fields, where they can express their unique perspectives and connect with others on a deeper level. This alignment between their emotional experiences and professional pursuits can lead to a sense of purpose and satisfaction. By integrating their artistic talents into their careers, they can create work that resonates with their values and contributes to their overall well-being.

Ultimately, the journey of channeling emotions into art is an integral part of personal development for Life Path 9 individuals. As they explore their creativity, they not only heal themselves but also empower others. This process encourages self-reflection, allowing them to uncover deeper layers of their identity and purpose. By embracing their emotional experiences and transforming them into art, Life Path 9 individuals can navigate their journeys with greater awareness, compassion, and a renewed sense of direction. Through this expressive journey, they unlock the potential within themselves and contribute significantly to the tapestry of human experience.

Chapter 6

Life Path 9 in Career and Work Environments

Ideal Career Paths

Life Path 9 individuals are often drawn to careers that align with their deep-seated values of compassion, creativity, and humanitarianism. They thrive in environments where they can make a significant impact, inspiring others and contributing to the greater good. Ideal career paths for Life Path 9 include roles in social work, counseling, and nonprofit organizations. These professions allow them to address societal issues, advocate for change, and provide emotional support to those in need. The fulfillment derived from these careers often stems from their innate desire to heal and uplift others, solidifying their role as catalysts for positive transformation in the lives they touch.

Creative expression serves as another vital pathway for Life Path 9 individuals. Careers in the arts, such as writing, music, and visual arts, provide an outlet for their rich inner worlds and emotional depth. These creative endeavors not only allow them to share their unique perspectives but also facilitate emotional healing for themselves and their audiences. Engaging in creative work can become a therapeutic process, enabling them to navigate their own life's challenges while inspiring others to do the same. Embracing their artistic talents can lead to a profound sense of purpose and fulfillment, further solidifying their connection to their Life Path.

In the realm of spiritual growth and development, Life Path 9 individuals often find themselves drawn to careers in holistic healing, coaching, and personal development. These roles allow them to assist others on their journeys toward self-discovery, emotional healing, and spiritual awakening. Whether through teaching mindfulness practices, offering life coaching, or facilitating workshops, they can guide others in unlocking their potential and navigating their own challenges. This alignment not only encourages their personal growth but also reinforces their commitment to fostering a more compassionate and understanding world.

Life Path 9 individuals may also find fulfillment in careers related to environmental advocacy and sustainability. Their strong sense of social justice and awareness of global issues often leads them to roles that focus on protecting the planet and promoting sustainable practices. Careers in this area allow them to utilize their creativity and problem-solving skills to address pressing environmental concerns, while also promoting a vision of a harmonious coexistence with nature. This alignment with their values reinforces their sense of purpose and enhances their ability to contribute to meaningful change.

Ultimately, the ideal career paths for Life Path 9 individuals are those that resonate with their core values of empathy, creativity, and service to humanity. By recognizing their unique gifts and how they can contribute to the world, they can choose careers that not only fulfill their personal aspirations but also align with their broader mission of healing and transformation. Embracing these paths enables Life Path 9 individuals to lead lives filled with purpose and meaning, making a lasting impact on the world around them.

Navigating Workplace Dynamics

Navigating workplace dynamics can be particularly nuanced for individuals on Life Path 9, who are typically characterized by their humanitarian instincts, creativity, and deep emotional awareness. In professional environments, these traits can manifest as a strong desire to contribute positively to the world while also seeking meaningful connections with colleagues. Life Path 9 individuals often find themselves in roles where they can make a difference, but this can also lead to challenges when faced with the complexities of workplace relationships and the demands of corporate culture. Understanding how these dynamics play out is essential for harnessing their full potential.

Effective communication is one of the cornerstones of navigating workplace dynamics. Life Path 9 individuals often possess a natural ability to empathize with others, allowing them to connect deeply with colleagues. However, this sensitivity can also lead to misunderstandings or emotional overwhelm in high-pressure environments. It is crucial for them to cultivate clear and assertive communication skills while remaining open to feedback. By establishing boundaries and expressing their needs, Life Path 9 individuals can create a healthier work environment that respects their emotional landscape while also promoting collaboration.

Collaboration is another key element in workplace dynamics for Life Path 9 individuals. Their innate desire to serve others often makes them exceptional team players. However, they may encounter difficulties when their vision for humanitarian efforts clashes with the goals of their organization. To navigate this, it is vital for them to seek roles or projects that align with their values. Finding common ground with colleagues and superiors can lead to innovative solutions that satisfy both the organization's objectives and their personal mission to make a difference. Emphasizing shared goals can foster a sense of unity that enhances overall productivity.

Conflict resolution is an inevitable aspect of any workplace, and for Life Path 9 individuals, the approach to resolving disputes can be deeply influenced by their emotional depth and desire for harmony. They may naturally gravitate toward mediation roles, striving to bring peace and understanding to conflicting parties. However, it is essential for them to recognize when to step back and allow others to resolve their issues independently. Developing skills in detachment and impartiality can help them navigate conflicts without becoming overly involved, thus preserving their emotional well-being while still contributing positively to the workplace atmosphere.

In conclusion, navigating workplace dynamics as a Life Path 9 individual involves a delicate balance of empathy, communication, collaboration, and conflict resolution. By harnessing their innate gifts while also being mindful of their emotional needs, they can thrive in various professional settings. Embracing these strategies not only enhances personal growth but also allows Life Path 9 individuals to fulfill their purpose of serving humanity, ultimately leading to a more meaningful and impactful career journey. Understanding these dynamics equips them to transform challenges into opportunities for growth, fostering both personal and collective success in their work environments.

Leadership and Teamwork

Leadership and teamwork are integral components in the journey of a Life Path 9 individual. As natural humanitarians, those on this path often find themselves in roles where they inspire and uplift others. Leadership for a Life Path 9 is less about authority and more about serving others and fostering a sense of community. They possess a unique ability to connect with diverse groups, making them effective leaders who can bring out the best in their team members. This innate sense of compassion allows them to lead with empathy, creating an environment where everyone feels valued and understood.

In teamwork, Life Path 9 individuals thrive when they can collaborate with others who share their vision for a better world. Their creative expression shines in group settings, where they can contribute innovative ideas that promote healing and growth. As they work alongside others, they often act as mediators, helping to resolve conflicts and encourage open communication. This ability to harmonize differing perspectives creates a cohesive unit that can tackle challenges effectively. Life Path 9 individuals are often catalysts for change, inspiring their teams to push beyond conventional boundaries and explore new ways of achieving their goals.

Moreover, the emotional healing journey of a Life Path 9 plays a significant role in their approach to leadership and teamwork. By embracing their own vulnerabilities and experiences, they develop a deeper understanding of the struggles faced by others. This insight enables them to approach leadership with a sense of humility and compassion, creating a safe space for their team to express their own challenges. In this nurturing environment, team members are encouraged to share their thoughts and feelings openly, leading to stronger bonds and increased trust within the group.

Balancing personal development with team dynamics is essential for Life Path 9 individuals. They must remain aware of their own emotional needs while also being attuned to the needs of their team. This dual focus allows them to cultivate their own spiritual growth while simultaneously elevating those around them. By fostering a culture of support and encouragement, Life Path 9 leaders can inspire their teams to pursue not only collective goals but also individual aspirations. This synergy creates a powerful force for positive change, as team members feel empowered to explore their unique gifts.

In conclusion, leadership and teamwork for Life Path 9 individuals are deeply intertwined with their purpose of serving humanity. Their ability to lead with empathy, foster collaboration, and promote emotional healing sets them apart as influential figures in any group setting. By embracing their roles as both leaders and team players, Life Path 9 individuals can unlock their full potential and help others do the same. In doing so, they contribute to a greater cause, finding meaning and fulfillment in their journey while making a significant impact on the world around them.

Chapter 7

Spiritual Growth and Development for Life Path 9

The Spiritual Journey

The spiritual journey of individuals on Life Path 9 is marked by a profound exploration of self and a deep connection to the universe. As compassionate humanitarians, those on this path often find themselves driven by a sense of purpose that transcends personal ambition. Their spiritual growth often involves embracing ideals of universal love, forgiveness, and service. This journey invites them to develop a broader perspective on life, seeing themselves as part of a greater whole while simultaneously acknowledging their unique contributions to humanity.

Emotional healing plays a crucial role in the spiritual journey of Life Path 9 individuals. They may encounter challenges that compel them to confront their past traumas, insecurities, and emotional wounds. Through this process, they learn to integrate their experiences, transforming pain into wisdom. This healing not only enhances their emotional well-being but also enriches their ability to empathize with others. As they navigate their own emotional landscape, they cultivate the resilience needed to support those around them, reinforcing their role as healers and nurturers.

Creative expression serves as a vital outlet for Life Path 9 individuals, allowing them to channel their spiritual insights into tangible forms. Whether through art, music, writing, or other creative endeavors, they find ways to communicate their understanding of the human experience. This creative process often becomes a spiritual practice in itself, as it connects them to their innermost thoughts and feelings while fostering a sense of community with others. By sharing their gifts, they inspire others on their own spiritual journeys, creating a ripple effect that extends far beyond their immediate circle.

In their professional lives, those on Life Path 9 often seek careers that align with their values and desire to make a difference. They may gravitate toward roles in non-profit organizations, social work, or the arts, where their compassionate nature can shine. However, balancing their idealism with the practical demands of work can be challenging. Through self-reflection and personal development strategies, they learn to navigate these tensions, ensuring that their careers not only fulfill their material needs but also resonate with their spiritual aspirations.

Ultimately, the spiritual journey of Life Path 9 individuals is about finding purpose and meaning in life. By embracing their unique gifts and confronting their challenges, they unlock a deeper understanding of themselves and their place in the world. This journey is not only about personal transformation but also about contributing to the collective healing of humanity. As they cultivate forgiveness, empathy, and love, they embody the essence of what it means to be a Life Path 9, paving the way for others to follow their lead in this shared journey toward enlightenment and fulfillment.

Practices for Inner Peace

For individuals on Life Path 9, the quest for inner peace can be a transformative journey that aligns with their inherent qualities of compassion, empathy, and creativity. These individuals often feel a deep connection to the world around them, which can lead to feeling overwhelmed by the suffering and challenges they observe. Thus, establishing practices that cultivate inner peace is essential for maintaining emotional balance and well-being. This chapter will explore various techniques that resonate with Life Path 9 individuals, helping them navigate their unique emotional landscapes while contributing positively to the greater good.

Mindfulness and meditation stand out as powerful tools for fostering inner peace. These practices encourage Life Path 9 individuals to turn inward, allowing them to connect with their thoughts and feelings without judgment. By integrating mindfulness into their daily routines, they can cultivate awareness of the present moment, reducing anxiety caused by past regrets or future worries. Regular meditation sessions can help them access a deeper sense of calm, enabling them to recharge emotionally and spiritually. This not only supports their personal growth but also enhances their capacity to be of service to others, which is a core aspect of their life journey.

Creative expression serves as another significant practice for achieving inner peace among Life Path 9 individuals. Engaging in art, music, writing, or other forms of creativity allows them to channel their emotions into something tangible and beautiful. This process can be incredibly therapeutic, providing an outlet for the intense feelings that often accompany their empathetic nature. By embracing their creativity, Life Path 9 individuals can transform pain into art, fostering healing for themselves and potentially inspiring others. This practice not only nurtures their own inner peace but also strengthens their connection to the wider community, as their creations resonate with the shared human experience.

Forgiveness is a crucial aspect of inner peace that Life Path 9 individuals must embrace. The tendency to carry emotional burdens can weigh heavily on their spirits, leading to feelings of resentment or unresolved pain. By consciously practicing forgiveness—both towards themselves and others—they can release these burdens and open their hearts to healing. This process may involve reflecting on past experiences, understanding the motivations behind others' actions, and ultimately choosing to let go of negativity. In doing so, they cultivate a sense of liberation and serenity, which empowers them to live more fully and authentically.

Lastly, establishing a routine that includes self-care and nurturing relationships plays a vital role in enhancing inner peace. Life Path 9 individuals often prioritize the needs of others, sometimes at the expense of their own well-being. By consciously setting aside time for self-care—whether through physical activities, relaxation, or social connections—they reinforce their emotional resilience. Surrounding themselves with supportive and like-minded individuals who share their values can also create a nurturing environment that fosters inner peace. Ultimately, integrating these practices into their lives can lead to profound emotional healing and personal growth, allowing Life Path 9 individuals to shine brightly on their journey of self-discovery and humanitarian efforts.

Connecting with Universal Consciousness

Connecting with Universal Consciousness invites Life Path 9 individuals to engage in a profound exploration of their spiritual essence and interconnectedness with all beings. Life Path 9 is often characterized by a deep sense of empathy and a desire to serve humanity. This inclination serves as a gateway to understanding the universal consciousness that binds us all. By tapping into this consciousness, Life Path 9 individuals can harness their unique gifts, fostering emotional healing not only within themselves but also extending compassion to others in their communities.

To connect with universal consciousness, it is essential for Life Path 9 individuals to cultivate mindfulness and presence. Practices such as meditation, journaling, and reflective contemplation can facilitate this connection, allowing for a clearer perception of the shared human experience. Through these practices, one can recognize the underlying threads of love and unity that weave through all life. This awareness not only enhances personal emotional healing but also empowers individuals to act from a place of understanding and compassion, which is vital in humanitarian efforts.

The creative expression is another powerful conduit for connecting with universal consciousness. Life Path 9 individuals often possess artistic talents that can serve as a medium for self-expression and emotional release. Engaging in creative activities—whether through art, music, writing, or other forms—can help bridge the gap between the individual self and the collective consciousness. By sharing their creativity, they not only honor their own journey but also resonate with others, fostering a sense of belonging and unity in the process.

In career and work environments, Life Path 9 individuals can embody the principles of universal consciousness by prioritizing collaboration over competition. They thrive in roles that allow for altruism and creativity, and by aligning their professional lives with their values, they can contribute positively to the workplace dynamic. This alignment not only enhances their job satisfaction but also encourages a culture of empathy and support among colleagues, reinforcing the interconnected nature of human experience.

Ultimately, connecting with universal consciousness is a transformative journey that inspires spiritual growth and personal development for Life Path 9 individuals. It allows them to transcend personal challenges and obstacles, fostering resilience and a deeper understanding of forgiveness. As they navigate their unique paths, they gain insights into their purpose and meaning in life, contributing to a greater collective awakening. By embracing this connection, Life Path 9 individuals not only unlock their own potential but also become catalysts for change in the world around them.

Chapter 8

Relationships and Compatibility for Life Path 9

Understanding Relationship Needs

Understanding relationship needs is a crucial aspect for individuals on Life Path 9, who often seek deeper connections and meaningful interactions. Life Path 9 individuals are characterized by their empathetic nature, humanitarian instincts, and a strong desire to contribute positively to the world. These traits influence their approach to relationships, making it essential to recognize and articulate their needs clearly. Understanding these needs not only fosters healthier partnerships but also enhances personal growth and emotional healing.

One primary need for Life Path 9 individuals is the desire for authenticity in their relationships. They thrive in environments where they can express their true selves without fear of judgment. This need stems from their inherent sensitivity and deep emotional awareness. When surrounded by authenticity, they feel validated and supported, allowing them to contribute their unique perspectives and creative expressions to the relationship. Partners who appreciate and encourage this authenticity help Life Path 9 individuals flourish, creating a strong bond built on trust and mutual respect.

Another significant aspect of relationship needs for Life Path 9 individuals is the necessity for emotional connection. They often seek partners who can engage with them on a deeper emotional level, sharing not just experiences but also vulnerabilities. This emotional depth allows them to heal from past traumas and encourages growth within the relationship. Life Path 9 individuals must communicate their emotional needs clearly to their partners, fostering an environment where both parties feel safe to explore their feelings and experiences together.

Additionally, Life Path 9 individuals have a strong inclination towards humanitarian efforts, which influences their relationship dynamics. They often seek partners who share their values and are committed to making a difference in the world. This alignment in purpose can strengthen their bond, as they work together towards common goals. Relationships that support and amplify this inclination not only nurture personal development but also create a powerful synergy that enhances both partners' sense of purpose and fulfillment.

Finally, understanding the need for balance between giving and receiving is vital for Life Path 9 individuals. They tend to be natural givers, often placing others' needs above their own. While this trait is admirable, it can lead to feelings of depletion if not managed properly. Life Path 9 individuals should actively cultivate relationships that encourage reciprocity, allowing them to receive the support and care they offer. By establishing boundaries and recognizing their own needs, they can create healthier, more sustainable relationships that honor their gifts while promoting mutual growth and healing.

Compatibility with Other Life Paths

Life Path 9 individuals are known for their deep sense of compassion, humanitarianism, and creativity. Their compatibility with other life paths can greatly enhance their journey toward self-discovery, allowing them to harness their unique gifts while also contributing positively to the lives of others. It is essential to understand that while Life Path 9 resonates with traits such as idealism, selflessness, and a desire to serve, this path can interact harmoniously with various other life paths, fostering growth, emotional healing, and supportive relationships.

When considering compatibility, Life Path 9 often finds a natural connection with Life Paths 2, 6, and 11. Life Path 2 individuals offer balance and diplomacy, complementing the empathic nature of Life Path 9. This pairing can create a nurturing environment, where both partners support each other emotionally and spiritually. Life Path 6, known for its nurturing and caring qualities, aligns well with the humanitarian aspects of Life Path 9. Together, they can create a loving atmosphere focused on service and community. Life Path 11, with its intuitive and visionary qualities, can inspire Life Path 9 to explore deeper spiritual realms, enhancing their creative expression and personal growth.

In contrast, Life Path 9 may encounter challenges when paired with Life Paths that embody more self-centered or materialistic traits, such as Life Path 1 or 8. While these paths bring ambition and leadership qualities, they can sometimes clash with the altruistic nature of Life Path 9. This doesn't mean that these relationships cannot work; rather, they require a conscious effort to bridge the differences. Life Path 9 individuals should be mindful of their own boundaries and ensure that their giving nature is reciprocated, fostering a balance that honors both partners' needs.

Creative expression is a central theme for Life Path 9, and their compatibility with other artistic paths, such as Life Path 3, can lead to powerful collaborations. Life Path 3 individuals, known for their creativity and sociability, can inspire Life Path 9 to channel their emotions into art, music, or writing. Together, they can explore innovative ideas and projects that have the potential to uplift and inspire others. Such partnerships not only enhance personal development but also align with Life Path 9's desire to make a difference in the world.

Ultimately, the journey of Life Path 9 is deeply intertwined with relationships and connections to others. By embracing compatibility with various life paths, individuals on this journey can unlock their potential for emotional healing and spiritual growth. Learning to navigate differences while celebrating shared values will lead to fulfilling partnerships that enhance their humanitarian efforts and creative endeavors. The exploration of these connections is a vital aspect of finding purpose and meaning, allowing Life Path 9 individuals to shine brightly in both personal and collective spheres.

Building Healthy Connections

Building healthy connections is essential for individuals on Life Path 9, as these connections serve as both a mirror and a support system throughout their journeys of self-discovery. Life Path 9 individuals often carry a deep empathy and compassion for others, which can sometimes lead to emotional exhaustion if they do not set healthy boundaries. Recognizing the importance of mutual respect and understanding in relationships is crucial for nurturing these connections. It is vital for Life Path 9 individuals to invest time in their relationships while also ensuring that they do not lose sight of their own needs and aspirations.

One of the key elements in building healthy connections is effective communication. Life Path 9 individuals may find themselves drawn to humanitarian efforts, advocating for causes that resonate with their values. This passion can sometimes manifest as a tendency to prioritize the needs of others over their own. By cultivating open and honest communication, they can express their thoughts and feelings without fear of judgment, fostering deeper connections that are built on trust and authenticity. This also includes active listening, which allows them to understand and validate the experiences of others while sharing their own.

In the context of emotional healing, building healthy connections can be transformative. Life Path 9 individuals often face challenges related to their past experiences, which can affect their ability to form lasting relationships. Engaging in supportive communities or groups that share similar interests can be a powerful way to heal old wounds and forge new bonds. These connections can provide a safe space for emotional expression, healing, and personal growth. By surrounding themselves with individuals who understand their journey, Life Path 9 individuals can cultivate a sense of belonging and acceptance.

Creative expression is another vital avenue for Life Path 9 individuals to connect with others. Whether through art, music, writing, or other forms of creativity, sharing their unique perspectives can lead to enriching interactions. These creative outlets not only help in personal expression but also serve as a bridge to connect with like-minded individuals. Collaborating on creative projects can foster teamwork and enhance interpersonal relationships, ultimately leading to a greater sense of community and shared purpose.

Lastly, as Life Path 9 individuals strive for spiritual growth, they must remain mindful of the importance of forgiveness within their connections. Holding onto past grievances can hinder personal development and impact relationships negatively. By embracing the power of forgiveness, they can release emotional burdens and open themselves to healthier, more fulfilling connections. This process not only benefits their relationships but also enhances their overall life experience, allowing them to live in alignment with their higher purpose and contribute positively to the world around them.

Chapter 9

Life Path 9 and Personal Development Strategies

Setting Personal Goals

Setting personal goals is an essential practice for individuals on Life Path 9, as it catalyzes the journey of self-discovery and personal growth. Life Path 9s are often characterized by their deep empathy, creativity, and a strong desire to contribute to the greater good. By establishing clear, personal goals, they can harness their innate abilities and direct their energies toward meaningful pursuits. These goals should reflect their values and aspirations, allowing them to align their daily actions with their broader vision for life.

One of the primary areas where Life Path 9 individuals can benefit from goal setting is in emotional healing. As natural healers, they often take on the emotional burdens of others, which can lead to personal challenges. Setting goals focused on self-care, mental health, and emotional resilience can empower them to prioritize their own well-being. This may include establishing routines that promote mindfulness, seeking therapeutic practices, or pursuing creative outlets that facilitate emotional expression. By committing to these goals, Life Path 9s can cultivate a healthier emotional landscape, ultimately enhancing their capacity to support others.

In the realm of humanitarian efforts, Life Path 9 individuals often feel a calling to make a difference in the world. Setting specific, actionable goals in this area can transform their aspirations into tangible outcomes. Whether it involves volunteering, starting a nonprofit, or advocating for social justice, defining clear objectives helps them channel their compassion and drive into impactful initiatives. These goals not only serve the community but also provide Life Path 9s with a profound sense of purpose, reinforcing their identity as agents of change.

Creative expression is another vital aspect of goal setting for Life Path 9 individuals. Their artistic inclinations can be a powerful tool for self-discovery and personal development. By setting goals related to creative projects, such as writing, painting, or music, they can explore their inner worlds and communicate their unique perspectives. These creative endeavors not only foster personal growth but also resonate with others, allowing Life Path 9s to connect and inspire through their work. Establishing goals in this domain encourages them to embrace their creativity as a legitimate and valuable pursuit.

Lastly, personal development strategies play a crucial role in the journey of Life Path 9 individuals. Setting goals that focus on enhancing skills, expanding knowledge, and fostering spiritual growth can lead to profound transformations. This may involve pursuing education, engaging in workshops, or exploring new philosophies that resonate with their spiritual beliefs. By committing to continuous growth, Life Path 9s can overcome obstacles and challenges that arise, finding resilience and strength in their journey. Ultimately, thoughtful goal setting empowers them to navigate their unique path with intention and clarity, unlocking the full potential of their Life Path 9 journey.

Developing Life Skills

Developing life skills is an essential aspect of the journey for individuals on Life Path 9. As natural humanitarians, those on this path often find themselves drawn to the service of others, which can sometimes lead to neglecting their own personal growth. It is crucial for Life Path 9 individuals to cultivate a robust set of life skills that not only enhance their ability to aid others but also foster their emotional healing and self-discovery. This growth can be achieved through a mindful approach to learning, self-reflection, and the intentional practice of new skills that align with their unique gifts.

One of the key life skills for Life Path 9 individuals is emotional intelligence. This includes the ability to recognize and manage one's own emotions as well as the emotions of others. Developing this skill can lead to deeper connections in relationships, improved communication, and a greater capacity for empathy. Life Path 9 individuals are often sensitive to the feelings of those around them, and honing emotional intelligence can help them navigate complex social dynamics and contribute to their humanitarian efforts. Workshops, books, and practices like mindfulness and journaling can serve as effective tools for enhancing emotional awareness.

Creative expression is another vital skill for those on Life Path 9. Engaging in creative pursuits not only nurtures the soul but also serves as a powerful outlet for processing emotions and experiences. Whether through art, music, writing, or other forms of creativity, Life Path 9 individuals can tap into their innate talents and share their unique perspectives with the world. This expression not only aids in personal development but can also inspire and uplift others, fulfilling the humanitarian aspect of their life purpose. Regular involvement in creative activities can significantly enhance their overall well-being and sense of fulfillment.

In professional settings, Life Path 9 individuals often excel in roles that allow for collaboration, innovation, and service. Developing skills such as leadership, teamwork, and conflict resolution can be particularly beneficial in navigating career environments. As natural leaders who strive for the greater good, honing these skills can empower Life Path 9 individuals to create meaningful change within their workplaces. Furthermore, embracing opportunities for continuous learning and growth can lead to career satisfaction and a sense of purpose, aligning their work with their life's mission.

Lastly, the ability to forgive and let go is a transformative life skill for those on Life Path 9. This path often involves overcoming challenges and obstacles that stem from past experiences, whether personal or collective. Learning to practice forgiveness—both towards oneself and others—can facilitate emotional healing and release the burdens of resentment that may hinder personal growth. This skill not only supports their own journey but also enhances their capacity to help others heal, embodying the essence of their humanitarian spirit. By prioritizing the development of these life skills, individuals on Life Path 9 can unlock their full potential, leading to a life rich in purpose, connection, and fulfillment.

Continuous Self-Improvement

Continuous self-improvement is an essential theme for individuals on Life Path 9, as it aligns with their innate desire for growth, healing, and contribution to the world. Life Path 9 individuals often embody the archetype of the humanitarian, driven by a need to make a difference in the lives of others. By embracing the practice of continuous self-improvement, they not only enhance their own lives but also amplify their capacity to serve and uplift those around them. This journey of personal evolution is not merely about achieving external success; it is about nurturing the inner self, fostering emotional resilience, and creating a deeper connection to one's purpose.

For those on this path, emotional healing plays a pivotal role in self-improvement. Life Path 9 individuals are often sensitive and empathetic, which can lead to emotional burdens if not addressed. Engaging in practices such as mindfulness, journaling, or therapy can facilitate the release of past traumas and allow for the integration of lessons learned. This emotional clarity is crucial for personal development, enabling Life Path 9 individuals to approach their relationships and humanitarian efforts with a renewed sense of compassion and understanding. As they heal, they become better equipped to support others, embodying the change they wish to see in the world.

Creativity is another vital component of continuous self-improvement for Life Path 9 individuals. Their imaginative spirit can be harnessed through various forms of creative expression, whether it be art, writing, music, or other mediums. Engaging in creative activities not only serves as a therapeutic outlet but also fosters a deeper understanding of self and the human experience. This creative journey allows for exploration and experimentation, encouraging Life Path 9 individuals to discover their unique gifts and share them with the world. By embracing their creative potential, they can inspire others and enhance their own sense of fulfillment.

In career and work environments, continuous self-improvement is equally important. Life Path 9 individuals thrive in roles that allow them to contribute positively to society, whether through nonprofit work, social advocacy, or creative industries. They are often drawn to careers that align with their values and passions. By seeking ongoing professional development, whether through training, mentorship, or networking, they can cultivate their skills and expand their impact. This commitment to growth not only benefits their career trajectory but also reinforces their sense of purpose and connection to the greater good.

Ultimately, the journey of continuous self-improvement for Life Path 9 individuals is intertwined with their spiritual growth and development. Embracing practices such as meditation, reflection, or community service can deepen their understanding of life's complexities and foster a sense of interconnectedness. As they navigate their path, they may encounter challenges and obstacles, but these experiences can serve as catalysts for growth and transformation. By cultivating a mindset focused on learning and self-betterment, Life Path 9 individuals can unlock their full potential, transforming their lives and the lives of those they touch.

Chapter 10

Life Path 9: Overcoming Challenges and Obstacles

Common Challenges Faced

Individuals on Life Path 9 often encounter a range of unique challenges that can impede their journey toward self-discovery and fulfillment. One significant challenge is the tendency to feel overwhelmed by the weight of the world's problems. Life Path 9 individuals are natural humanitarians, deeply empathetic, and driven by a desire to make a positive impact. However, this sensitivity can lead to emotional fatigue, as they may absorb the pain and struggles of those around them. It is essential for these individuals to recognize the importance of self-care and setting boundaries to protect their emotional well-being while still engaging in meaningful humanitarian efforts.

Another common challenge faced by Life Path 9 individuals is a struggle with self-acceptance and self-worth. Often, they may feel like they are not living up to their full potential or that their contributions are insufficient. This internal conflict can manifest as feelings of inadequacy or self-doubt, which can hinder their creative expression and overall personal development. By embracing their unique gifts and understanding that their worth is inherent, Life Path 9 individuals can begin to foster a more positive self-image and channel their creativity into impactful endeavors.

Relationships can also pose a challenge for those on Life Path 9. Their deep emotional sensitivity and desire for connection can sometimes lead to misunderstandings or feelings of isolation. While they often attract others with their compassion and warmth, they may struggle to find partners or friends who truly understand their depth and complexity. Open communication and vulnerability are essential for Life Path 9 individuals to foster healthy relationships. By sharing their experiences and feelings, they can build stronger connections that honor their emotional needs and promote mutual understanding.

Navigating career paths can be another hurdle for Life Path 9 individuals, who often seek meaningful work that aligns with their humanitarian values. However, they may find themselves in environments that prioritize profit over purpose, leading to frustration and dissatisfaction. In order to thrive, they must seek out careers that not only allow them to express their creativity but also fulfill their desire to contribute positively to society. Emphasizing teamwork and collaboration can help Life Path 9 individuals find fulfillment in their professional lives while remaining true to their values.

Finally, the journey of personal growth for Life Path 9 individuals often involves confronting unresolved emotional wounds and embracing the power of forgiveness. Past experiences can create barriers to emotional healing and hinder their ability to move forward. By addressing these challenges and practicing forgiveness—both for themselves and others—Life Path 9 individuals can unlock profound emotional healing. This process ultimately allows them to step into their purpose with clarity and confidence, further enhancing their capacity to contribute to the greater good and find meaning in their lives.

Strategies for Overcoming Difficulties

Strategies for overcoming difficulties are essential for individuals on Life Path 9, as they often encounter unique challenges related to their empathetic nature and humanitarian inclinations. One effective strategy is the practice of emotional healing through self-reflection and mindfulness. Life Path 9 individuals frequently absorb the emotional energies of those around them, which can lead to overwhelm. By engaging in regular self-reflection, such as journaling or meditative practices, they can process their feelings, distinguish between their emotions and those of others, and cultivate a sense of inner peace. Mindfulness techniques, such as deep breathing and grounding exercises, can also help them stay present, reducing anxiety and enhancing emotional resilience.

Another crucial strategy involves harnessing creative expression as a tool for coping and growth. Life Path 9 individuals often possess a rich creative potential that can serve as an outlet for their emotions and thoughts. Engaging in artistic endeavors, whether through writing, painting, music, or other forms of creativity, allows them to channel their feelings constructively. This creative process not only provides relief but also fosters a deeper understanding of their experiences. By embracing their artistic inclinations, Life Path 9 individuals can transform difficulties into opportunities for expression, ultimately leading to personal growth and healing.

Additionally, cultivating supportive relationships is vital for overcoming challenges. Life Path 9 individuals are natural caregivers and often prioritize the needs of others, sometimes at the expense of their own well-being. Establishing boundaries within relationships is essential for maintaining balance. They should seek connections with those who understand their emotional depth and can reciprocate support. By surrounding themselves with like-minded individuals who share their humanitarian values and respect their need for space and reflection, Life Path 9 individuals can create a nurturing environment that fosters resilience during difficult times.

Engaging in humanitarian efforts can also serve as a powerful strategy for overcoming personal difficulties. Life Path 9 individuals are often drawn to causes that promote social justice and compassion. By volunteering their time and skills to support those in need, they not only contribute positively to the world but also gain perspective on their challenges. This shift in focus can alleviate feelings of helplessness and empower them to make meaningful contributions. The act of helping others often results in a profound sense of fulfillment, reinforcing their sense of purpose and connection to the greater human experience.

Lastly, embracing the power of forgiveness is a transformative strategy for overcoming difficulties on Life Path 9. Many individuals on this path may carry emotional burdens related to past experiences or relationships. Learning to forgive—both themselves and others—can be a liberating process. It allows them to release negative emotions and move forward with a clearer mindset. Practicing forgiveness does not mean condoning hurtful actions; rather, it involves acknowledging pain, learning from it, and choosing to let go. This powerful act can lead to emotional healing and a renewed sense of purpose, enabling Life Path 9 individuals to navigate life's challenges with grace and resilience.

Transforming Obstacles into Opportunities

Transforming obstacles into opportunities is a fundamental aspect of the journey for individuals on Life Path 9. This life path is intrinsically linked to humanitarian efforts, emotional healing, and a deep-seated desire to contribute to the greater good. Individuals on this path often face significant challenges that can initially appear overwhelming. However, these obstacles serve a dual purpose: they are gateways to personal growth and catalysts for meaningful change in the world. Embracing the transformative power of adversity allows Life Path 9 individuals to unlock their potential and develop resilience, ultimately leading to greater emotional and spiritual fulfillment.

The key to transforming obstacles into opportunities lies in the ability to shift perspective. Life Path 9 individuals are often naturally empathetic and compassionate, qualities that can be harnessed to reframe challenges as learning experiences. For example, a setback in career advancement might be perceived not simply as a failure but as an opportunity to reassess personal goals and priorities. By adopting a mindset that views challenges as stepping stones rather than stumbling blocks, individuals can cultivate a sense of empowerment that facilitates personal and professional growth. This perspective not only aids in overcoming individual hurdles but also inspires those around them to embrace their own challenges.

Emotional healing is another crucial component of this transformation. Life Path 9 individuals often carry emotional baggage from past experiences, which can manifest as obstacles in their present lives. Engaging in practices such as meditation, journaling, or therapy can help individuals process these emotions and release limiting beliefs. This healing journey fosters a deeper understanding of oneself and the motivations behind one's actions, paving the way for personal development. As individuals learn to navigate their emotional landscapes, they become better equipped to turn their obstacles into opportunities for connection, creativity, and community engagement.

In the context of relationships and compatibility, transforming obstacles into opportunities can lead to deeper, more meaningful connections. Life Path 9 individuals often prioritize the well-being of others, sometimes at the expense of their own needs. Learning to communicate openly about challenges allows for the development of more authentic relationships where vulnerability is met with understanding. These authentic connections not only enrich personal lives but also create a network of support that encourages collective growth. As individuals on Life Path 9 embrace their challenges, they can inspire others to do the same, fostering a culture of resilience and compassion.

Ultimately, the journey of transforming obstacles into opportunities aligns seamlessly with the overarching themes of Life Path 9: purpose, meaning, and service. By recognizing that every challenge carries within it the seeds of opportunity, individuals can embark on a path of self-discovery that not only enhances their own lives but also contributes to the well-being of the world around them. This transformation is not merely about overcoming difficulties; it is about leveraging those experiences to create a legacy of hope, healing, and humanitarianism. In doing so, Life Path 9 individuals honor their innate gifts and fulfill their role as catalysts for positive change.

Chapter 11

Life Path 9 and the Power of Forgiveness

Understanding Forgiveness

Understanding forgiveness is an essential aspect of emotional healing, particularly for individuals on Life Path 9. Those on this path often experience deep emotional connections with others and possess a strong sense of empathy. This heightened sensitivity can lead to feelings of hurt and disappointment, making the ability to forgive crucial for personal growth. Forgiveness is not merely an act of letting go but a transformative process that allows individuals to release the burdens of resentment and anger. By understanding the nature of forgiveness, Life Path 9 individuals can unlock deeper levels of compassion and empathy, both for themselves and others.

At the core of forgiveness lies the recognition that holding onto grievances can hinder emotional and spiritual development. Life Path 9 individuals are often called to assist others and contribute to humanitarian efforts. However, unresolved emotional issues can create barriers to fully engaging in these pursuits. By embracing forgiveness, they can clear the emotional clutter that weighs them down, enabling them to focus on their higher purpose. This process allows for the cultivation of a more profound sense of peace, empowering them to serve others without the burden of past grievances.

Forgiveness also plays a significant role in relationships for Life Path 9 individuals. Their natural inclination towards nurturing can sometimes lead to taking on the emotional pain of others. This dynamic can result in feelings of overwhelm or the tendency to hold onto past hurts. To foster healthier relationships, it is vital for Life Path 9 individuals to practice forgiveness, not only towards others but also towards themselves. By acknowledging their imperfections and mistakes, they can create a more compassionate inner narrative, which, in turn, enhances their connections with others.

In the context of career and work environments, forgiveness can unlock pathways to collaboration and innovation. Life Path 9 individuals often thrive in roles that involve creativity and humanitarianism. However, workplace conflicts and misunderstandings can arise, potentially stifling their creativity and sense of purpose. By actively engaging in forgiveness, they can create a more harmonious work environment, fostering collaboration and open communication. This shift not only enhances their own work experience but also contributes positively to the collective energy of the workplace.

Ultimately, understanding forgiveness is a pathway to personal development for Life Path 9 individuals. It allows them to confront their own challenges and obstacles with a renewed perspective. Embracing forgiveness as a powerful tool for emotional healing facilitates spiritual growth, enabling them to align more closely with their life purpose. As they learn to forgive themselves and others, they discover the freedom to express their creativity fully and engage in meaningful relationships, all while contributing to the greater good of humanity.

The Role of Forgiveness in Healing

Forgiveness serves as a pivotal element in the healing journey for individuals on Life Path 9, who are often characterized by their deep empathy and commitment to humanitarian causes. This path, marked by a desire to serve others, can lead to emotional burdens when one becomes entangled in the pain of others or experiences personal grievances. The act of forgiving releases these burdens, allowing Life Path 9 individuals to reclaim their emotional energy and transform their experiences into wisdom. This process is not just about absolving others; it is fundamentally about liberating oneself from the shackles of resentment and anger that can impede personal growth.

In the context of emotional healing, forgiveness fosters a space for introspection and self-discovery. Life Path 9 individuals, often sensitive and introspective, may dwell on past hurts, whether they stem from interpersonal relationships or societal injustices. By embracing forgiveness, they can navigate through their emotions more effectively, recognizing that healing begins within. This inner journey often leads to powerful insights that contribute to their personal development. As they forgive, they not only heal themselves but also enhance their capacity to empathize with others, deepening their connections and reinforcing their role as compassionate humanitarians.

Forgiveness also plays a crucial role in creative expression for Life Path 9 individuals. Many find solace in artistic endeavors, using creativity as a medium to process their emotions. When they practice forgiveness, they unlock the flow of inspiration and creativity that may have been stifled by unresolved pain. The act of letting go allows for a renewed sense of purpose in their creative pursuits, enabling them to produce work that resonates deeply with others. This creative output often reflects their journey of healing, serving as a testament to the transformative power of forgiveness.

In professional environments, Life Path 9 individuals can benefit significantly from fostering a culture of forgiveness. In workplaces that emphasize collaboration and support, the ability to forgive can lead to healthier relationships and improved productivity. When conflicts arise, practicing forgiveness encourages open communication and a focus on collective goals rather than individual grievances. This not only enhances team dynamics but also aligns with the Life Path 9's intrinsic desire to contribute positively to the world around them, making workplaces more harmonious and effective.

Ultimately, forgiveness is a crucial step in the spiritual growth of Life Path 9 individuals. It allows them to transcend personal grievances and align more closely with their higher purpose. By understanding that forgiveness is not just a gift to others but a vital component of their own healing process, they can cultivate an inner peace that empowers them to pursue their humanitarian goals with renewed vigor. In this journey of self-discovery, embracing forgiveness becomes a powerful tool for transforming pain into purpose, enabling them to impact the world meaningfully.

Practicing Forgiveness in Daily Life

Practicing forgiveness in daily life is an essential aspect for individuals on Life Path 9, as it aligns closely with their innate humanitarian instincts and emotional healing journeys. Forgiveness serves as a powerful tool for releasing the burdens of past grievances, allowing Life Path 9 individuals to cultivate inner peace and clarity. Embracing forgiveness enables them to move forward, not only for their own well-being but also for the greater good of those around them. In this context, forgiveness can be seen as a pathway to personal development, helping to unlock the potential that Life Path 9 embodies.

To effectively practice forgiveness, Life Path 9 individuals must first engage in self-reflection. This process helps them understand their emotions and the impact that unresolved conflicts have on their lives. By acknowledging their feelings, they can begin to identify the root causes of resentment or anger. This introspective journey fosters emotional healing, allowing them to recognize that holding onto negative emotions hinders their ability to express their creativity and participate in humanitarian efforts. Embracing forgiveness thus becomes an act of self-care, facilitating personal growth and enhancing their capacity for empathy.

In relationships, the practice of forgiveness can significantly improve connections with others. Life Path 9 individuals often prioritize harmony and understanding, making it essential for them to navigate conflicts with grace. By choosing to forgive, they foster an environment of trust and openness, which is vital for deepening relationships. This act of releasing past grievances not only strengthens bonds but also enhances their ability to collaborate in creative endeavors and community service. The ripple effect of forgiveness in relationships ultimately contributes to a more compassionate and supportive world, aligning perfectly with the Life Path 9 mission.

Forgiveness also plays a crucial role in the career and work environments of Life Path 9 individuals. In professional settings, conflicts and misunderstandings are inevitable, but practicing forgiveness can transform these challenges into opportunities for growth. By letting go of grudges, Life Path 9 individuals can cultivate a positive workplace culture that encourages collaboration and innovation. This not only elevates their professional experiences but also reinforces their commitment to making meaningful contributions to society. In this way, forgiveness becomes a powerful catalyst for success in both personal and professional realms.

Finally, the act of forgiving empowers Life Path 9 individuals to connect with their higher purpose. As they release the burdens of resentment, they create space for spiritual growth and development. This journey of forgiveness invites them to embrace their role as compassionate leaders and visionaries who inspire others. By embodying forgiveness, they not only heal themselves but also serve as beacons of hope for those around them, illustrating the profound impact of unconditional love and acceptance. Ultimately, practicing forgiveness in daily life aligns seamlessly with the Life Path 9 journey, enriching their quest for purpose and meaning in life.

Chapter 12

Life Path 9: Finding Purpose and Meaning in Life

Defining Personal Purpose

Defining personal purpose is a transformative journey, especially for those on Life Path 9. As individuals who resonate with humanitarian ideals, empathy, and a strong desire to contribute to the greater good, defining personal purpose is not merely an exercise in self-reflection but a crucial step toward aligning one's life with their inherent gifts. Life Path 9 individuals often grapple with questions of meaning and fulfillment, making it essential to explore what truly drives them. This exploration often leads to a deeper understanding of their unique role in the world, allowing them to harness their strengths for positive impact.

At the core of personal purpose for Life Path 9 individuals lies the concept of service. This path emphasizes compassion and a commitment to helping others, which can manifest in various ways. Whether through community involvement, creative expression, or humanitarian efforts, identifying how one can contribute meaningfully to society is vital. By reflecting on their passions and interests, Life Path 9 individuals can uncover their purpose, often finding that it revolves around uplifting others and fostering a sense of unity. This realization can be incredibly empowering, as it aligns personal fulfillment with the broader mission of making the world a better place.

Emotional healing also plays a significant role in defining personal purpose. Life Path 9 individuals may face challenges stemming from their deep sensitivity and empathy, leading to emotional turmoil or burnout. It is crucial for them to engage in self-care practices that promote healing, allowing them to navigate their own emotions effectively. As they heal, they can better articulate their purpose, often discovering that their experiences of pain and healing can serve as a powerful catalyst for helping others on similar journeys. This connection between personal healing and purpose underscores the importance of self-awareness and emotional intelligence in the lives of Life Path 9 individuals.

Creative expression is another avenue through which Life Path 9 individuals can define their personal purpose. Many on this path are naturally drawn to artistic pursuits, whether it be through writing, music, visual arts, or other forms of creativity. Engaging in creative endeavors not only allows for self-exploration but also provides an outlet for sharing their insights and emotions with the world. By embracing their creativity, Life Path 9 individuals can communicate their understanding of life's complexities, inspiring others and fostering a sense of community. This creative expression often becomes intertwined with their sense of purpose, reinforcing the idea that their artistic gifts can serve a higher calling.

Ultimately, defining personal purpose for Life Path 9 individuals is a dynamic and holistic process that encompasses service, emotional healing, and creative expression. By understanding their unique gifts and the challenges they face, Life Path 9 individuals can cultivate a purposeful existence that resonates deeply with their values. This journey invites them to explore their identity and aspirations while making meaningful contributions to the world. Through this exploration, they not only unlock their potential but also illuminate the path for others seeking similar clarity and fulfillment.

Aligning Actions with Values

Aligning actions with values is a crucial practice for individuals on Life Path 9, as it not only reflects personal integrity but also enhances their journey toward self-discovery and fulfillment. Life Path 9 individuals often feel a deep calling to serve humanity, and when their actions resonate with their core values, they experience a profound sense of purpose. This alignment fosters an environment in which their creative expressions can flourish, allowing them to channel their talents into humanitarian efforts that reflect their ideals. By understanding and articulating their values, Life Path 9 individuals can make conscious choices that elevate their lives and those around them.

To begin this alignment process, it is essential for Life Path 9 individuals to engage in self-reflection. This introspective journey involves examining personal beliefs, passions, and the motivations that drive their actions. Journaling, meditation, or even engaging with a trusted friend or mentor can facilitate this exploration. By identifying what truly matters to them, they can pinpoint their values—whether it be compassion, creativity, justice, or healing. This clarity serves as a guiding light, enabling them to navigate their life choices and ensure they remain true to themselves in every aspect of their lives.

In professional settings, aligning actions with values takes on a transformative role for Life Path 9 individuals. They often thrive in careers that allow them to express their humanitarian spirit, such as in social work, the arts, or community organizing. When their work resonates with their values, they not only contribute positively to society but also experience greater job satisfaction and emotional well-being. Conversely, when there is a disconnect between their values and their professional actions, it can lead to frustration and burnout. Seeking roles that embody their values can pave the way for a fulfilling career that integrates their passions with their purpose.

Relationships are another critical area where Life Path 9 individuals must strive for alignment between values and actions. Healthy relationships are built on mutual respect and understanding, and by communicating their values openly, Life Path 9 individuals can attract like-minded partners and friends. This alignment also fosters deeper connections, as it encourages authenticity and vulnerability. In romantic relationships, for instance, sharing and respecting each other's values can lead to a more harmonious and supportive partnership, allowing both individuals to grow and evolve together.

Ultimately, aligning actions with values is an ongoing practice that contributes significantly to the spiritual growth and emotional healing of Life Path 9 individuals. This alignment not only enhances their self-esteem and confidence but also reinforces their purpose in life. By consistently evaluating and adjusting their actions to be in harmony with their values, they cultivate a life rich with meaning and fulfillment. This journey of alignment encourages not just personal development but also a broader impact on the world, as Life Path 9 individuals embody the change they wish to see, inspiring others to do the same.

The Journey to Fulfillment

The journey to fulfillment for individuals on Life Path 9 is one marked by deep introspection and a profound commitment to service. Life Path 9 individuals are often characterized by their humanitarian instincts and a desire to make the world a better place. This innate drive compels them to explore their emotions and experiences, seeking healing not only for themselves but also for those around them. As they navigate the complexities of their emotional landscapes, they uncover layers of resilience and compassion that become instrumental in their quest for fulfillment. This journey is not merely about personal satisfaction; it is about creating a ripple effect of positive change that extends far beyond their immediate surroundings.

Emotional healing plays a pivotal role in the journey to fulfillment for Life Path 9 individuals. Many struggle with the weight of their sensitivities, often feeling overwhelmed by the suffering they observe in the world. This heightened empathy can lead to emotional turmoil, making it essential for them to engage in practices that foster healing. Techniques such as mindfulness, journaling, and even creative expression serve as vital tools in their healing arsenal. By acknowledging and processing their emotions, they can transform their personal pain into a source of strength, allowing them to support others more effectively in their healing journeys.

In the realm of humanitarian efforts, Life Path 9 individuals find a profound sense of purpose and meaning. Their desire to contribute to the greater good often leads them toward careers in social work, non-profit organizations, or community activism. These paths allow them to align their work with their values, providing a sense of fulfillment that transcends monetary success. Additionally, their natural ability to inspire and lead others makes them invaluable in collaborative efforts aimed at addressing social issues. As they engage in these pursuits, they not only fulfill their own needs for purpose but also uplift those around them, creating a shared sense of accomplishment and hope.

Creative expression is another vital aspect of the journey to fulfillment for Life Path 9. These individuals often possess unique artistic talents that serve as an outlet for their emotions and experiences. Whether through writing, painting, music, or other forms of art, they can channel their feelings into creations that resonate deeply with others. This creative process not only brings personal satisfaction but also offers a means of connection with the wider world. By sharing their art, they can inspire others to embark on their own journeys of self-discovery and healing, further amplifying their impact on society.

Ultimately, the journey to fulfillment for Life Path 9 individuals is a multifaceted process that integrates emotional healing, humanitarian efforts, and creative expression. As they face challenges and obstacles, their capacity for forgiveness and understanding becomes crucial. This journey is not just about personal growth; it is about embracing a larger vision of interconnectedness and shared humanity. By unlocking their gifts and embracing their path, Life Path 9 individuals can illuminate their own lives while guiding others toward a more fulfilled existence, creating a legacy of compassion and purpose that endures.